Philip Bourke Marston, Louise Chandler Moulton

Garden Secrets

Philip Bourke Marston, Louise Chandler Moulton

Garden Secrets

ISBN/EAN: 9783337090036

Printed in Europe, USA, Canada, Australia, Japan

Cover: Foto ©Andreas Hilbeck / pixelio.de

More available books at **www.hansebooks.com**

GARDEN SECRETS.

BY

PHILIP BOURKE MARSTON,

AUTHOR OF "SONG-TIDE," "ALL-IN-ALL," "WIND-VOICES," "FOR
A SONG'S SAKE, AND OTHER STORIES," ETC.

With Biographical Sketch

BY LOUISE CHANDLER MOULTON.

It seemed each sun-thrilled blossom there
Beat like a heart among the leaves.
D. G. ROSSETTI.

BOSTON:
ROBERTS BROTHERS.
1887.

MY GARDEN.

O my Garden, full of roses,
    Red as passion and as sweet,
Failing not when summer closes,
    Lasting on through cold and heat!.

O my Garden, full of lilies,
    White as peace and very tall,
In your midst my heart so still is,
    I can hear the least leaf fall!

O my Garden, full of singing,
    From the birds that house therein,
Sweet notes down the sweet day ringing,
    Till the nightingales begin!

O my Garden, where such shade is,
    O my Garden, bright with sun, —
O my loveliest of Ladies,
    Of all gardens sweetest one!

CONTENTS.

———◆———

PHILIP BOURKE MARSTON:

𝔄 𝔖𝔨𝔢𝔱𝔠𝔥.

----◆----

"Around the vase of Life at your slow pace
He has not crept, but turned it with his hands,
And all its sides already understands."

IT is not alone to the loving partiality
of friendship that the life of Philip
Bourke Marston must seem at once one of
the most tragic and the most interesting of
the literary records of the last half of the
nineteenth century. Seldom, surely, has
so much genius been wedded to so much
sorrow; seldom has work so noble been
achieved under difficulties so great. His
keen pain was not infrequently his inspira-
tion, and the chords from which he drew
his music were heart-strings. What wonder that his melodies were oftenest written
in a minor key?

He was born into poetry, one might almost say. Far away back in the Elizabethan days one John Marston was a poet and a dramatist, and Dr. Westland Marston, the father of our poet, has himself written poems of very great beauty, though he is more widely known as a dramatist than as a poet pure and simple. Dr. Marston's first play, "The Patrician's Daughter," was produced at the Drury Lane Theatre, under Macready's management, in 1842, its author being at that time only twenty-three years of age ; and it has been succeeded by many other notable dramatic productions.

Philip's mother was a woman of quiet and domestic tastes, who lived in and for her husband and her children; but she was also a woman of much cultivation, — a good critic, a fine linguist, a loving reader of the best books, — exactly fitted to be the blessing of poet-husband and poet-son. His two sisters, Ciceley and Eleanor (afterwards the wife of the poet Arthur O'Shaughnessy) were both older than him-

self; and this one son was the darling of
the household.

Philip James Bailey, the author of " Fes-
tus," was his godfather, for whom he was
in part named; and Miss Muloch, afterwards Mrs. Craik, was his godmother. He
was a beautiful child; and it was to him,
in his fascinating babyhood, that Miss
Muloch addressed her well-known lyric,
commencing: —

> " Look at me with thy large brown eyes,
>   Philip, my king,
> For round thee the purple shadow lies
> Of babyhood's regal dignities."

Alas for the large brown eyes! When
he was three years old he received a blow
·which was, as his father has often told me,
the cause of his blindness. He was play-
ing with some other little boys, and his
eyes were especially sensitive at the time,
in consequence of belladonna, which had
been administered as a preventive of· scar-
let fever. The blow, which accidentally hit
one eye, inflamed it, and that inflammation
was communicated to the other; and he

soon became what I should have called
blind, save that he said to me with energy,
" No, I was *not* blind then. I could n't read,
of course, or see the faces of people, but I
could see the tree-boughs waving in the
wind, and I could see the pageant of sun-
set in the West, and the glimmer of a fire
upon the hearth; and oh! it was such a dif-
ferent thing from the days that came afterwards, when I could not see anything!"

How many tales he has told me of his
darkened, dream-haunted childhood! He
began very early to feel the full pain of
his loss of vision. He fell in love, when
he was not more than nine or ten years
old, with a beautiful young lady, and went
through all a lover's gamut of joys and
pains; and sometimes the torture of not
being able to behold the beauty of his
adored was so extreme that he used to
dash his head against the wall, in a sudden
mad longing to be done at once with life
and sorrow. Yet the love of life was keen
in him, and his earliest childhood was
haunted by dreams of future fame which

should make people acknowledge that, though blind, his soul yet saw unshared visions.

He could not play with other boys, and he listened to wonderful conversations of grown men and women instead. He began to compose almost before he had left off pinafores, and at an incredibly early age dictated a three-volume tale, which his mother wrote out for him and preserved for a long time as a literary curiosity. Before he was fourteen the same loving hand had written out for him several manuscript books of verses, some of them by no means destitute of real poetic merit.

His *life* was his education. His home was the resort of men like Browning, Dickens, Thackeray, and all the group of intellectual giants of that time; and every day's guests were his unconscious teachers. He was fourteen, I think, when he first met Swinburne, who was just then the idol of his boyish worship. At that time — so wonderful was his memory — he actually knew by heart the whole of the first series

of "Poems and Ballads." He was taken to
visit his demigod, and entered the sacred
presence with a heart beating almost to
suffocation; and went home feeling that
his hopes and dreams had been, for once,
fulfilled. To the very end of his days
Swinburne's friendship was a pride and
joy to him and I have seen scores of
letters in which the elder poet gave to the
younger praise so cordial and so earnest
that one might wear it proudly as a wreath
of immortelles. Later on he grew to
know intimately Dante Gabriel Rossetti;
of whom he has often spoken to me as
the one man he had ever met for whom
"it was possible to feel a devotion as
romantic and as worshipful as a man feels
for an adored woman." Like Swinburne,
Rossetti ardently admired and encouraged
the young poet's genius. To carry to this
adored friend poems copied in the clear,
graceful hand of his mother, and to hear
the elder poet read and comment on them,
was one of the high delights which helped
to reconcile the inspired boy to his dark-

ened fate. I have seen Rossetti's numerous
letters ; and I think one might have courage
to bear almost any calamity in life, fortified
by such letters from such a man, — *almost*
any calamity ; but not such weight of woes
as overwhelmed this sad-fated poet, whom,
as he himself said in one of his strongest
sonnets, " the gods derided."

When he was scarcely twenty his mother
died. Hitherto she had written out all
his poems, sympathized with his ambi-
tions, shared his dreams, and been at
once friend and mother. Her loss was
the second great and irremediable mis-
fortune of his life. He mourned for her
with the passionate intensity characteristic
of his nature ; but after a brief time there
seemed to be for him a promise of con-
solation. He loved and was beloved by
Miss Mary Nesbit, to whom he became
engaged. A harrowing but utterly mis-
taken story has been told of her sudden
death in the midst of health and without
any previous warning. The facts were
quite otherwise. About the time of the

betrothal Miss Nesbit developed symptoms of consumption. The disease progressed very rapidly for three months; but the end was neither unforeseen nor especially sudden. The blow which thus shattered the young poet's hopes of a shared future and a happy domesticity to console him for his darkened life was heavy indeed. Previously to this loss—in 1871 — Marston's first volume, "Song-Tide, and Other Poems," had appeared, and had met with a marked success. The group of sonnets called " Song-Tide " were those in which, like Petrarch, he had chanted his lady's praises; and he was able to give to his betrothed, before her death, the first copy of this Book of Love. Just then — while there was still hope that she might live — just then, if ever, was the tide of Marston's life at the full. Poets and critics alike praised his work. I have seen letters on letters of praise from Swinburne and Rossetti, and in one of them the latter wrote: " Only yesterday evening I was reading your ' Garden Secrets ' to

William Bell Scott, who fully agreed with
me that it is not too much to say of them
that they are worthy of Shakspeare in his
subtlest lyrical moods." On this height
of achievement and of joy stood Philip
Bourke Marston at twenty-one. He was
reckoned by the masters of song as among
their high kindred; readers were clamor-
ing for a second edition of his book; the
girl to whom he had given his young love
had not shrunk from clasping hands with
him in his darkness. But still "the gods
derided him."

In November, 1871, his betrothed died;
and then the last flickering flame of light
went out from his sad eyes. Was it that
so many tears had quenched it? Ciceley,
who loved him as sisters seldom love, gave
herself to his service in that hour of his
supreme need even more completely than
his mother had done. She wrote for him,
read to him, lived in and for him. She
had decided literary gifts of her own;
but she devoted herself so wholly to her
brother that she sought no theatre for

their display, and published only two stories. From the time of their mother's
death Philip and Ciceley lived together in
London, save when they went away for
some pleasant outing, — usually to France,
but once to Italy, the "woman-country,"
the dream-land of poets, the home of art,
Eight years afterwards Philip wrote, —

> " Oh, how fleet,
> How fair with dreams accomplished, heavenly sweet,
> Was that our sovereign month in Italy!"

To breathe Italian air, to stand in Dante's
Florence, to drift in gondolas at Venice
between ancient palaces that seemed to
sleep and dream above tideless waters, — it
all touched his imagination quite as keenly
as if his eyes had seen it. With some
subtler vision than ours, he beheld this
beauty that was as the beauty of a dream.
Those golden weeks were a memory of
joy which seemed never to lose its fresh
zest for all the rest of his life.

In 1872 Marston formed a close intimacy
with Oliver Madox Brown, son of the well-
known artist Ford Madox Brown, and

himself a painter of promise and an author already of noble and memorable performance, though he died before he was twenty. How often I have heard Marston speak of him as his friend of friends, whose like could never come again. In 1874 this gifted genius and charming and beloved young man died, in his turn, after a brief illness; and again those blind eyes burned with the hopeless tears which mourn the dead.

Before young Brown died, Marston had prepared for the press his second volume of poems, " All-in-All." This, with the exception of one poem to his sister, was the poetic record of his grief for his dead sweetheart. It was too uniformly sad and too monotonous in theme to achieve so speedy a success as " Song-Tide" had secured; but it contained some of its author's most noble and stately poems. It was very soon after the publication of " All-in-All" in 1874 that " Scribner's Monthly" (now " The Century") printed the first of Marston's numerous contributions to the American

Press. As he wrote so much for America
and had so many American friends, he
used to keep the American flag in his
room, and playfully to declare himself " a
natural American citizen."

Among the American friends whom he
devotedly loved were Mrs. Laura Curtis
Bullard, — whose tender helpfulness and
subtle comprehension of his moods especially endeared her to him, — the Southern
poet Paul Hamilton Hayne, who was for
years his constant correspondent, and E. C.
Stedman, whom he warmly appreciated
both as poet and as critic. Among his
other American friends were Whittier, —
who had written to and of him in the most
cordial manner, — Mrs. Margaret J. Preston, Mrs. S. M. B. Piatt, Richard Watson
Gilder, and Mrs. Z. B. Gustafson.

It was in the summer of 1876 that my
own friendship with him began. I met
him first on the first day of that year's
July. It was at a sort of authors' night at
a well-known London house; and I knew
that the blind poet would be among the

guests, — the one, indeed, whom I most desired to meet, as I had previously been much interested in his poems.

I soon perceived him, standing beside his sister Ciceley, — a slight, rather tall man of twenty-six, very young looking even for his age. He had a wonderfully fine brow. His brown eyes were still beautiful in shape and color. His dark-brown hair and beard had glints of chestnut, and all his coloring was rich and warm. His was a singularly refined face, with a beautiful expression when in repose; keenly sensitive, but with full, pleasure-loving lips, that made one understand how hard his limitations must be for him to whom beauty and pleasure were so dear. At that time the color came and went in his cheeks as in those of a sensitive girl. His sister soon grew to be my intimate friend; and I knew the whole family so well that Philip's past life became as familiar to me as it could be to any one who had not shared it. His companionship was a revelation to me of the possible completeness of intellectual sympathy. In reading to him I can scarcely recall a time when our tastes or judgments differed. If I said, "How beautiful that is!" he would answer: "Yes, I was waiting for you to say that." One could hardly hope to meet twice in a lifetime such kinship of the spirit.

I had known him and his sister but a few days more than two years, when, on July 28, 1878, Ciceley called upon me at my rooms. Dr. Marston and Philip were away in France, and she spoke of them very tenderly that morning. She complained, when she came in, of an intense headache; and after a little while I made her lie down, to see what rest would do for her. She grew worse; and when the doctor came, he pronounced her illness apoplexy. My name was the last word on her faithful lips; and in the mid-afternoon of that long July day she died. Quite unaware of her death, — since we did not know where to find them with a telegram, — and while she was still awaiting burial, her father and brother returned. On this

crushing sorrow I cannot linger; its full
bitterness I shared. I think it was the
cruellest bereavement that had ever come
to our poet. When his mother, his betrothed, and his friend died, he still — as
he used often to say — had Ciceley; but
when she left him there remained for him
no such constant and consoling presence.
His other sister was married, and therefore
was not in his daily life at all; and at that
time, even, she herself was a chronic in-
valid. His father was his one closest tie:
but many sorrows had saddened Dr. Marston and broken his health; and there was
no one to be to Philip what Ciceley had
been as reader, amanuensis, and constant,
untiring companion. It was the year before Ciceley's death, 1877, in which, to
gratify a whim of mine, the well-known
novelist R. E. Francillon cast Philip's horoscope. Mr. Francillon is a loving stu-
dent of all mystic lore; and has studied
astrology, by way of amusing himself,
until he has become a thorough proficient
in its mysteries. As a sort of test of the

clear-seeing of the stars, I persuaded him
to cast and carefully to write out the
horoscope of the blind poet; and in this
manuscript — which I still have in my pos-
session — he prophesied, several times over,
the death of its subject in 1887. One
never believes in such prophecies until
after their fulfilment; but I look back
now to see with wonder how many pre-
dictions even besides this final one that
horoscope contained, and how strangely
they have been fulfilled.

After the loss of his sister, Marston en-
larged the circle of his intimate friends.
He became devotedly attached to the
young poets Mary Robinson, William
Sharp, and Herbert Clarke. Mr. Church-
ill Osborne, of Salisbury, was another com-
paratively recent but very dear friend.
Iza Duffus Hardy had been the tender,
helpful, sister-like friend of all his life.
Theodore Watts, the beloved friend of
Rossetti and of Swinburne, — himself poet,
critic, and romancer, — has written most
tenderly of the dead poet in " The Athe-

næùm." These and many others clung
to Philip devotedly until the last; and the
world out of which he has gone will never
be quite the same again for these his
friends. In 1883 Marston published his
latest volume of poems, entitled " Wind-
Voices." It was an immediate success.
Roberts Brothers, of Boston, sold every
copy of the edition they imported, and
the London publishers sold every copy
they had retained, — the last of them at a
considerable prémium; for, unfortunately,
the book was not stereotyped, and was
soon out of print on both sides of the At-
lantic. Since its publication the author's
strength of body has seemed, year by
year, to decline. He told me many times
how brief he felt would be his remaining
days; but I could never believe it, for he
seemed, after all, too full of life to die.
How gay he was, when he had anybody
with whom to make merry, how full of
wit and fun and laughter! I felt that
he *must* go on living; and yet, knowing
how sad was his heart down under the

laughter, I was not surprised by this passage in one of his letters: " You will miss me, perhaps, when I am gone, but you must not mourn for me. I think few lives have been so deeply sad as mine, though I do not forget those who have blessed it."

During the August of 1886 he had a serious attack of illness, — something of the nature of brain-fever; and one of his delusions was, that outside his window in Brighton, where he was staying with his father — out of this window, which looked upon a stone-paved yard, he could see an ocean stretching broad and blue, and on it ships, with great white sails set, going always to America. He had longed much to come here, and had always felt sure that he would come some day. So when his disordered brain had visions of these white-winged ships sailing where he longed to go, he used to smile in his pain and his weakness, and say they would stop for him soon. Ah! what other ship has stopped for him since then, and over what unknown sea, to what far port, has he been borne?

I saw him after this illness, at the end of September. He was much changed from his old self, and his once fine memory had greatly failed. He remembered every incident of eight or ten years ago with an almost photographic minuteness, and recurred to long-past conversations and old jests; but he forgot the events of yesterday, the appointments of to-morrow. " I am horribly broken up by that illness," he used to say to me, " and I don't know why I should want to live; but I dread that mystery beyond. If I only *knew!*" Still, I did not once think that he would die. All through the winter of 1886–1887 his letters were unutterably sad, and very much briefer than usual, because — as he was always saying — he felt too weak to sit up at his type-writer. Sometimes he would write: "I hope you will be coming soon, else I shall never see you again." And once he wrote: "I feel that I said my last good-by to you that 4th of October

when we parted at the Euston Station. I
shall be gone — somewhere — before you
come again. The stony streets will be
here, and the bells that drive me mad will
ring; but *I* shall be gone. You will miss
me sometimes, I think, you and a few
others; and perhaps people will be sorry
when they remember how dark and lonely
was the life I lived here." That passage
was in one of his mid-winter letters; and
he wrote similar ones again and again.
How they come back to me now, — vain
cries out of the dark! At the time I
thought them only the expression of a
transient weakness, and looked tranquilly
forward to finding him better in the spring.
" If I *could* only sleep," he wrote, in letter
after letter; " I try everything, but rest
will not come. Is there anything in all
the world so good as sleep? " And now
" sleep wraps him round."

Alas, how bitterly we who loved him
know that we shall never see his like
again! As his friend Clarke wrote of him:
"He had a positive genius for friendship,

and drew together all sorts and conditions of men, who would never have otherwise met, and who could have agreed on no single subject except their attachment to him."

His friend William Sharp, who has edited since his death a collection of his tales, speaks of him, in the Memoir which prefaces that volume, as " possessed of an occult, magnetic quality of attraction which few people could resist. Wherever he went he made would-be friends, and without any apparent effort to please he seemed to exercise a pleasant fascination over all who came in contact with him; and down to his last days he was in company cheerful and animated, often merry, and always genial."

And his friend Osborne wrote to me of him in a private letter: " He had the most potent personality and the strongest power of fascination I have ever met with in any man."

The leading daily and weekly London papers have sounded his praises over the grave where what was mortal of him lies

deaf to all words of ours. Sonnets and
poems — at least a score of them — have
been written to his beloved memory; his
portrait has been engraved for the London " Graphic " and the " Illustrated London News;" notes of loving sympathy
have poured in on the father, sole sur-
vivor of all his household, who sits alone
in his bereavement and desolation. But *he*
whom so many loved, whom so many now
conspire to honor, *he* has gone on beyond
our ken, and is wiser than we all.

It was the last of January when he ex-
perienced what seemed like a slight shock
of paralysis. The first of February he
telegraphed to his friend Herbert Clarke
to come to him, for he was very ill. Clarke
went, and found him able to speak only
with the greatest difficulty; but he man-
aged to say that he wanted to live, and
hoped he should get better. After that
day until his death he never spoke at all.
His father wrote me that sometimes his
vain attempts to make himself understood
were agonizing. But at other times he
would be quiet, and seem to understand

all that was said to him; and when absent
friends were spoken of, a sweet and tender
smile would flicker round his speechless
lips. He hardly seemed to grow worse at
all during the last week. Indeed, on Sun-
day, February 13, there was more hope
for him than at any time after he was
seized with his fatal illness. But — to quote
his father's words in a letter to me — " On
Monday morning, at about 9.45, he alarmed
the nurse by a slight palpitation, gave one
or two sighs, and was gone. He almost
slept into eternity." On Friday, Feb. 18,
1887, he was buried in Highgate Cemetery.
Miss Hardy writes: " I saw his face just
before the coffin-lid closed on it. The
seal of peace was there. It was a calm
more utter than that of sleep, — marble-
still, serene." Another friend writes:
" Philip looked wonderfully transfigured
and most beautiful, his dark hair and beard
contrasting with the pure pallor of his face
— that peaceful face! " A cruel sleet was
falling when they laid him under the damp
sods at Highgate. His coffin was heaped
with loving tributes of flowers from many

a friend, and two white camellias were laid, inside, upon his heart. Bitter tears fell for him — and fall still; for he was not of those who die and are forgotten.

The world will not let his work die out of remembrance, or cease to be grateful for the rich gifts his too-short life bequeathed; but we, to whom he was personally so dear, what can the world's praise of him do towards comforting our sorrow? The very house he lived and died in must be haunted, it seems to me, forever by his pain; and as he himself wrote: —

> " Must this not be, that one then dwelling here,
>   Where one man and his sorrows dwelt so long,
>   Shall feel the pressure of a ghostly throng,
> And shall upon some desolate midnight hear
>   A sound more sad than is the pine-tree's song,
> And thrill with great, inexplicable fear ? "

Yes, it *must* count for something that these long woes are over, and that somewhere, " beyond these voices, there is Peace."

LOUISE CHANDLER MOULTON.

Garden Secrets.

—⬥—

THE ROSE AND THE WIND.

THE ROSE AND THE WIND.

DAWN.

THE ROSE.

WHEN, think you, comes the Wind,
  The Wind that kisses me and is so kind?
Lo, how the Lily sleeps ! her sleep is light.
Would I were like the Lily, pale and white !
Will the Wind come?

THE BEECH.

Perchance for thee too soon.

THE ROSE.

If not, how could I live until the noon?
What think you, Beech-tree, makes the Wind
    delay?
Why comes he not at breaking of the day?

THE BEECH.

Hush, child ! and, like the Lily, go to sleep.

THE ROSE.

You know I cannot.

THE BEECH.

Nay, then, do not weep.

[*After a pause.*]

Thy lover comes ; be happy, now, O Rose !
He softly through my bending branches goes.
Soon he shall come, and thou shalt feel his kiss.

THE ROSE.

Already my flushed heart grows faint with bliss.
Love, I have longed for you through all the night.

THE WIND.

And I to kiss your petals warm and bright.

THE ROSE.

Laugh round me, Love, and kiss me ; it is well.
Nay, have no fear ; the Lily will not tell.

MORNING.

THE ROSE.

'T was dawn when first you came ; and now the
sun
Shines brightly, and the dews of dawn are done.
'T is well you take me so in your embrace,
But lay me back again into my place ;
For I am worn, perhaps with bliss extreme.

THE WIND.

Nay, you must wake, Love, from this childish
dream.

THE ROSE.

'T is you, Love, who seem changed ; your laugh
is loud,
And 'neath your stormy kiss my head is bowed.
O Love, O Wind, a space will not you spare?

THE WIND.

Not while your petals are so soft and fair.

THE ROSE.

My buds are blind with leaves, they cannot see ;
O Love, O Wind, wilt thou not pity me?

EVENING.

.   THE BEECH.

O Wind ! a word with you before you pass :
What did you to the Rose, that on the grass
Broken she lies, and pale, who loved you so?

THE WIND.

Roses must live and love, and winds must blow.

THE DISPUTE.

THE DISPUTE.

THE GRASS.

I FELT upon me, as she passed, her feet.

THE BEECH.

'Neath my green shade she sheltered in the heat.

A ROSE.

She plucked me as she passed, and in her breast
Wore me, and I was to her beauty prest.

THE WIND.

And now ye lie neglected, withering fast ;
And the Grass withers too ; and when have past
These golden summer days, O Beech, no more
She'll sit beneath thy shade.   But I endure,
To kiss her when I will.   So, more than ye,
Am I made blest in my felicity.

WHAT THE ROSE SAW.

WHAT THE ROSE SAW.

THE ROSE.

O LILY sweet! I saw a pleasant sight.

THE LILY.

Where saw you it, and when?

THE ROSE.

Here, when the Night
Lay calmly over all and covered us,
And no wind blew, however tremulous,
I heard afar the light fall of *her* feet,
And murmur of her raiment soft and sweet.

THE LILY.

What said she to thee when she came anear?

THE ROSE.

No word; but o'er me bent till I could hear
The beating of her heart, and feel her blood

Swell to a blossom that which was a bud.
Alas ! I have no words to tell the bliss
When on my trembling petals fell her kiss ;
Sweeter than soft rain falling after heat,
Or dew at dawn, was that kiss, soft and sweet.
Then fell another shadow on the ground,
And for a little space there was no sound.
I knew who stood beside her, saw his face
Shining and happy in that happy place ;
I knew not what they said ; but this I know,
They kissed and passed : where think you they
       did go?

THE GARDEN'S LOSS.

THE GARDEN'S LOSS.

A LILY.

HE will not speak to us again ;
No more the sudden summer rain
Will fall from off his trembling leaves :
Even the scentless Tulip grieves.
Ah me ! the loud noise of that night,
And that fierce blaze of blinding light
That slew him in the midst of bliss —
Reach out, O Rose ! and let us kiss.

THE ROSE.

He was a friend to all indeed ;
Even the wild, unlovely Weed
Loved him and clove unto his root :
When next winds blow he shall be mute.

THE LILY.

He was the noblest of all trees.

A TULIP.

Your sorrow cannot bring you ease.

4

THE LILY.

Still we *must* mourn so great a one.

THE ROSE.

I would the summer-time were done !
The birds we loved sang in his boughs,
And in his branches made their house.
All graciously he bowed and swayed ;
And when of winds we were afraid,
How tenderly his boughs he moved, —
A loving tree, and well beloved.

AN ELM.

He was a noble tree and vast ;
His branches revelled in the blast :
I always took him for our king.
Yet better that he was so slain,
In midst of his loved wind and rain,
Than some sharp axe should lay him low.

THE ROSE.

Better !   But now I only know
He shall not speak again to me —
Nor, Lily, shall he speak to thee.

BEFORE AND AFTER FLOWERING.

BEFORE AND AFTER FLOWERING.

BEFORE.

FIRST VIOLET.

L O, here how warm and dark and still it is !
        Sister, lean close to me, that we may kiss.
Here we go rising, rising ; but to where ?

SECOND VIOLET.

Indeed I cannot tell, nor do I care,
It is so warm and pleasant here.   But hark !
What strangest sound was that above the dark ?

FIRST VIOLET.

As if our sisters all together sang ,—
Seemed it not so ?

SECOND VIOLET.

                More loud than that it rang ;
And louder still it rings, and seems more near.

Oh, I am shaken through and through with fear !
Now in some deadly grip I seem confined ! —
Farewell, my sister ! Rise and follow and find.

FIRST VIOLET.

From how far off those last words seemed to
    fall !
Gone where she will not answer when I call !
How lost? How gone? Alas ! this sound above
    me :
" Poor little Violet, left with none to love thee ! "
And now it seems I break against that sound !
What bitter pain is this that binds me round?
This pain I press into? Where have I come?

AFTER.

A CROCUS.

Welcome, dear sisters, to our fairy home !
They call this Garden, and the time is Spring.
Like you, I have felt the pain of flowering ;
But oh ! the wonder and the deep delight
It was to stand here, in the broad sunlight,
And feel the wind flow round me cool and kind ;
To hear the singing of the leaves the wind
Goes hurrying through ; to see the mighty trees,
Where every day the blossoming buds increase !

At evening, when the shining sun goes in,
The gentler lights we see, and dews begin,
And all is still beneath the quiet sky,
Save sometimes for the wind's low lullaby.

FIRST TREE.

Poor little flowers !

SECOND TREE.

What would you prate of now?

FIRST TREE.

They have not heard ; I will keep still.   Speak low.

FIRST VIOLET.

The trees bend to each other lovingly.

CROCUS.

Daily they talk of fairer things to be.
Great talk they make about the coming Rose,
The very fairest flower, they say, that blows,
Such scent she hath ; her leaves are red, they say,
And fold her round in some divine, sweet way.

FIRST VIOLET.

Would she were come, that for ourselves we
  might
Have pleasure in this wonder of delight !

CROCUS.

Here comes the laughing, dancing, hurrying rain :
How all the trees laugh at the wind's light strain !

FIRST VIOLET.

We are so near the earth, the wind goes by
And hurts us not ; but if we stood up high,
Like trees, then should we soon be blown away.

SECOND VIOLET.

Nay ; were it so, we should be strong as they.

CROCUS.

I often think how nice to be a tree ;
Why, sometimes in their boughs the stars I see.

FIRST VIOLET.

Have you seen that ?

CROCUS.

        I have, and so shall you.
But hush ! I feel the coming of the dew.

NIGHT.

SECOND VIOLET.

How bright it is ! the trees how still they are !

CROCUS.

I never saw before so bright a star
As that which stands and shines just over us.

FIRST VIOLET (*after a pause*).

My leaves feel strange and very tremulous.

CROCUS AND SECOND VIOLET TOGETHER.

And mine, and mine !

FIRST VIOLET.

O, warm, kind Sun, appear !

CROCUS.

I would the stars were gone, and day were here !

JUST BEFORE DAWN.

FIRST VIOLET.

Sisters ! No answer, sisters ?   Why so still ?

ONE TREE TO ANOTHER.

Poor little Violet, calling through the chill
Of this new frost which did her sister slay,
In which she must herself, too, pass away !
Nay, pretty Violet, be not so dismayed ;
Sleep only on your sisters sweet is laid.

FIRST VIOLET.

No pleasant Wind about the garden goes, —
Perchance the Wind has gone to bring the Rose.
O sisters ! surely now your sleep is done.
I would we had not looked upon the sun.
My leaves are stiff with pain.   O cruel night !
And through my root some sharp thing seems to
    bite.
Ah me ! what pain, what coming change is this?

(*She dies.*)

FIRST TREE.

So endeth many a Violet's dream of bliss.

THE ROSE'S DREAM.

THE ROSE'S DREAM.

I.

O SISTERS ! when last night so well you slept,
    I could not sleep ; but through the silent
        air
I looked upon the white moon, shining where
No scent of any rose can reach, I know.
And as I looked adown the path there crept
A little trembling, restless Wind, and lo !
As near it came, I said : " O little Breeze
That hast no strength wherewith to stir the trees !
What dost thou in this place ? "   It only sighed,
And paused a little ere it thus replied : —

II.

" I am the Wind that comes before the rain
Which, even now, bears onward from the west, —
The rain that is as sweet to you as rest.
When all the air about the day lies dead,
And the incessant sunlight grows a pain,
Then by the cool rain are you comforted.

O happy Rose, that shall not live to see
This summer garden altered utterly,
You know not of the days of snow and ice,
Nor know the look of wild and wintry skies."

III.

Then passed the Wind ; but left me very sad,
For I began to think of days to come,
Wherein the sun should fail and birds grow dumb,
And how this garden then should look, indeed.
And as I thought of all, such fear I had
I cried to you, asleep, though none would heed.
And so I wept, though none might see me weep,
Till came the Wind again, and bade me sleep,
And sang me such a small, sweet song that soon
I fell asleep while looking on the moon.

IV.

And as I slept I dreamed a fearful dream.
It seemed to me that I was standing here :
The sky was sunless, and I saw anear
All you, my sisters, lying dead and crushed.
I could not hear the music of the stream
That runs hard by, when suddenly there rushed
A giant Wind adown the garden walk,
And all the great old Trees began to talk

And cried : "What does the Rose here ?   Bid her
    go,
Lest buried she should be in coming snow."

V.

I strove to move away, but all in vain ;
And, flying, as it passed me cried the Wind :
"O foolish little Rose, and art thou blind ?
Dost thou not see the snow is coming fast ?"
And all the swaying Trees cried out again :
"O foolish Rose, to tarry till the last !"
Then came a sudden whirl, a mighty noise,
As every tree that lives had found a voice ;
And I was borne away, and lifted high
As birds that dart in summer through the sky.

VI.

And then the great Wind fell away ; and so
I felt that I was whirling down and down,
Past Trees that strove, with branches bare and
    brown,
To catch me as I fell ; and all they cried :
"She must be buried in the cold deep snow ;
Ah, would she had like other roses died !"
Then, as I thought to drop, I woke to find
The cool rain falling on me, and the Wind

Singing a rainy song among the trees,
Wherein the birds were building at their ease.

VII.

FIRST FLOWER.

A fearful dream indeed, and such an one
As well may make you sad for days to come.

SECOND FLOWER.

A sad, strange dream !

THE ROSE.

Why is the Lily dumb !

THE LILY.

Too sad the dream for me to speak about !

THE ROSE.

I fear this night the setting of the sun.

A TREE.

Nay, when the sun goes in, the stars come out.
You shall not dream, Rose, such a dream again ;
Forget it now in listening to the rain.

THE ROSE.

I would the Wind had never talked to me
Of things that I shall never live to see !

THE FLOWER AND THE HAND.

THE FLOWER AND THE HAND.

I.

JUST AFTER NIGHTFALL.

I HEARD a whisper of Roses,
   And light white Lilies laugh out :
"Ah ! sweet when the evening closes,
   And stars come looking about ;
How cool and good it is to stand,
Nor fear at all the gathering hand !"

II.

" Would I were red !" cried a White Rose.
   " Would I were white !" cried a Red one ;
" No longer the light Wind blows,
   He went with the dear, dead Sun.
Here we forever seem to stay ;
And yet a Sun dies every day."

III.

A LILY.

"The Sun is not dead, but sleeping,
    And each day the same Sun wakes ;
But when Stars their watch are keeping,
    Then a time of rest he takes."

MANY ROSES TOGETHER.

"How very wise these Lilies are !
They must have heard Sun talk with Star ! "

IV.

FIRST ROSE.

"Pray, then, can you tell us, Lilies,
    Where slumbers the Wind at night,
When the Garden all round so still is,
    And brimmed with the Moon's pale light ! "

A LILY.

"In branches of great trees he rests."

SECOND ROSE.

"Not so ; they are too full of nests."

V.

FIRST ROSE.

" *I* think he sleeps where the grass is ;
    He there would have room to lie.
The white Moon over him passes ;
    He wakes with the dawning Sky."

MANY LILIES TOGETHER.

" How very wise these Roses seem,
Who think they know, and only dream ! "

VI.

FIRST ROSE.

" What haps to a gathered flower ? "

SECOND ROSE.

" Nay, sister, now who can tell ?
Not one comes back for an hour
    To say it is ill or well.
I would with such an one confer,
To know what strange things chanced to her."

VII.

FIRST ROSE.

"Hush ! hush ! now the Wind is waking —
  Or *is* it the Wind I hear?
My leaves are thrilling and shaking —
  Good-by ; I am gathered, my dear !
Now, whether for my bliss or woe,
I shall know what the plucked flowers know ! "

GARDEN FAIRIES.

GARDEN FAIRIES.

KEEN was the air, the sky was very light,
    Soft with shed snow my garden was, and
        white ;
And walking there, I heard upon the night
        Sudden sound of little voices, —
        Just the prettiest of noises.

It was the strangest, subtlest, sweetest sound ;
It seemed above me, seemed upon the ground,
Then swiftly seemed to eddy round and round ;
        Till I said : " To-night the air is
        Surely full of garden fairies."

And all at once it seemed I grew aware
That little shining presences were there,
White shapes and red shapes danced upon the
        air ;
        Then a peal of silver laughter ;
        And such singing followed after

As none of you, I think, have ever heard.
More soft it was than note of any bird, —
Note after note, most exquisitely deferred,
  Soft as dew-drops when they settle
  In a fair flower's open petal.

"What are these fairies?" to myself I said ;
For answer, then, as from a garden's bed,
On the cold air, a sudden scent was shed, —
  Scent of lilies, scent of roses,
  Scent of Summer's sweetest posies.

And said a small sweet voice within my ear :
"We flowers that sleep through winter, once a
   year
Are by our flower queen let to visit here,
  That this fact may duly flout us, —
  Gardens can look fair without us.

" A very little time we have to play ;
Then must we go, oh ! very far away,
And sleep again for many a long, long day,
  Till the glad birds sing above us,
  And the warm Sun comes to love us.

" Hark what the roses sing; now, as we go ! "
Then very sweet and soft, and very low, —
A dream of sound across the garden snow, —
    Came the sound of Roses singing
    To the Lily-bell's faint ringing.

ROSES' SONG.

" Softly sinking through the snow,
  To our winter rest we go ;
  Underneath the snow to house
  Till the birds be in the boughs,
  And the boughs with leaves be fair,
  And the sun shine everywhere.
  Softly through the snow we settle,
  Little Snowdrops press each petal.
  Oh ! the snow is kind and white,
  Soft it is, and very light ;
  Soon we shall be where no light is,
  But where sleep is, and where night is, —
  Sleep of every wind unshaken
  Till our summer bids us waken."

Then toward some far-off goal that singing drew,
Then altogether ceased ; more steely blue
The blue stars shone ; but in my spirit grew
    Hope of summer, love of roses,
    Certainty that sorrow closes.

SUMMER CHANGES.

SUMMER CHANGES.

SANG the Lily and sang the Rose
   Out of the heart of my garden close :
"O joy, O joy of the summer tide ! "
Sang the Wind, as it moved above them :
" Roses were sent for the Sun to love them,
   Dear little buds, in the leaves that hide ! "

Sang the Trees, as they rustled together :
" O the joy of the summer weather !
   Roses and Lilies, how do you fare ? "
Sang the Red Rose, and sang the White :
" Glad we are of the sun's large light,
   And the songs of the birds that dart through
     the air."

Lily and Rose and tall green Tree,
Swaying boughs where the bright birds be,
   Thrilled by music and thrilled by wings,

How glad they were on that summer day !
Little they recked of cold skies and gray,
 Or the dreary dirge that a Storm-Wind sings !

Golden butterflies gleam in the sun,
Laugh with the flowers, and kiss each one ;
 And great bees come, with their sleepy tune,
To sip their honey and circle round ;
And the flowers are lulled by that drowsy sound,
 And fall asleep in the heart of the noon.

A small white cloud in a sky of blue :
Roses and Lilies, what will they do ?
 For a wind springs up and sings in the trees.
Down comes the rain ; the garden's awake :
Roses and Lilies begin to quake,
 That were rocked to sleep by the gentle breeze.

Ah, Roses and Lilies ! Each delicate petal
The wind and the rain with fear unsettle —
 This way and that way the tall trees sway ;
But the wind goes by, and the rain stops soon,
And smiles again the face of the noon,
 And the flowers grow glad in the sun's warm ray

Sing, my Lilies, and sing my Roses,
With never a dream that the summer closes.
But the Trees are old ; and I fancy they tell,
Each unto each, how the summer flies :
They remember the last year's wintry skies ;
But that summer returns the Trees know well.

6

THE LONELY ROSE.

THE LONELY ROSE.

" TO a heaven far away
     Went the Red Rose when she died."
So I heard the White Rose say,
     As she swayed from side to side
          In the chill October blast.
          In the garden leaves fall fast ;
          This of roses is the last :

Said the White Rose : " O my Red Rose !
     O my Rose so fair to see !
When, like thee, I am a dead rose,
     Shall *I* in that heaven be ? "
          Oh, the dread October blast !
          In the garden leaves fall fast ;
          This of roses is the last.

" From that heavenly place, last night,
     To me in a dream she came,

Stood there in the pale moonlight ;
  And she seemed, my Rose, the same."
    Oh, the bleak October blast !
    In the garden leaves fall fast ;
    This of roses is the last.

"Only it may be, perchance,
  That her leaves were redder grown,
And they seemed to thrill and dance,
  As by gentler breezes blown."
    Oh, the sad October blast !
    In the garden leaves fall fast ;
    This of roses is the last.

" And she told me, sweetly singing,
  Of that heavenly place afar,
Where the air with song is ringing,
  Where the souls of blossoms are."
    Hark, the wild October blast !
    In the garden leaves fall fast ;
    This of roses is the last.

" And she bade me not to fail her,
  Nor to lose my heart for fear,

When I saw the skies turn paler
  With the sickness of the year, —
    I should be beyond the blast,
    And the dead leaves falling fast,
    In that heavenly place at last."

WIND–GARDENS.

WIND–GARDENS.

MIDWAY between earth and sky,
  There the wild wind-gardens lie, —
Tossing gardens, secret bowers,
Full of songs and full of flowers,
Wafting down to us below
Such a fragrance as we know
Never yet had lily or rose
That our fairest garden knows.

Oh, those gardens dear and far,
Where the wild wind-fairies are! —
Though we see not, we can hearken
To them when the spring skies darken,
Singing clearly, singing purely
Songs of far-off Elf-land, surely,
And they pluck the wild-wind posies,
Lilies, violets, and roses,

Each to each the sweet buds flinging,
Fostering, tending them, and singing.
The sweet scent, like angels' pity,
Finds us, even in the city,
Where we, toiling, seek as treasures
Dull earth's disenchanting pleasures.
Oh, the gales, with wind-flowers laden,
Flowers that no mortal maiden

In her breast shall ever wear !
Flowers to wreathe Titania's hair,
And to strew her happy way with,
When she marries some wind-fay with!
O wind-gardens ! where such songs are,
And of flowers such happy throngs are,
Though your paths.I may not see,
Well I know how fair they be.

ROSES AND THE NIGHTINGALE.

ROSES AND THE NIGHTINGALE.

IN my garden it is night-time,
But a still time and a bright time ;
For the Moon rains down her splendor,
And my garden feels the wonder
Of the spell which it lies under
In that light so soft and tender.

While the Moon her watch is keeping,
All the Blossoms here are sleeping,
And the Roses sigh for dreaming
Of the bees that love to love them
When the warm sun shines above them
And the butterflies pass gleaming.

Could one follow Roses' fancies
When the night the garden trances,
Oh, what fair things we should chance on !
For to Lilies and to Roses,
As to us, soft sleep discloses
What the waking may not glance on.

But hark ! now across the moonlight,
Through the warmness of the June night,
From the tall Trees' listening branches,
　　Comes the sound, sustained and holy,
　　Of the passionate melancholy,
Of a wound which singing stanches.

Oh, the ecstasy of sorrow
Which the music seems to borrow
From the thought of some past lover
　　Who loved vainly all his lifetime,
　　Till death ended peace and strife-time,
And the darkness clothed him over !

Oh, the passionate, sweet singing,
Aching, gushing, throbbing, ringing,
Dying in divine, soft closes,
　　Recommencing, waxing stronger,
　　Sweet notes, ever sweeter, longer,
Till the singing wakes the Roses !

Quoth the Roses to the singer :
" Oh, thou dearest music-bringer,
Now our sleep so sweetly endeth,
　　Tell us why *thy* song so sad seems,
　　When the air is full of glad dreams,
And the bright moon o'er us bendeth."

Sang the Singer to the Roses :
" Love for you my song discloses ;
Hence the note of grief it borrows."
    Quoth the Roses : " Love means pleasure."
    Quoth the Singer : " Love's best measure
Is its pure attendant sorrows."

7

THY GARDEN.

-

THY GARDEN.

I.

PURE moonlight in thy garden, sweet, to-
    night,
  Pure moonlight in thy garden, and the breath
Of fragrant roses.   O my heart's delight !
    Wed thou with Love, but I will wed with
        Death.

Peace in thy garden, and the passionate song
    Of some last nightingale that sings in June !
Thy dreams with promises of love are strong,
    And all thy life is set to one sweet tune.

Love wandering round thy garden, O My Sweet !
    Love walking through thy garden in the night ;
Far off I feel his wings, I hear his feet,
    I see the eyes that set the world alight.

My sad heart in thy garden strays alone,
  My heart among all hearts companionless ;
Between the roses and the lilies thrown,
  It finds thy garden but a wilderness.

Great quiet in thy garden, now the song
  Of that last nightingale has died away ! .
Here jangling city chimes the silence wrong,
  But in thy garden perfect rest has sway.

Dawn in thy garden, with the faintest sound, —
  Uncertain, tremulous, awaking birds, —
Dawn in thy garden, and from meadows round,
  The sudden lowing of expectant herds.

Light in thy garden, faint and sweet and pure ;
  Dim noise of birds from every bush and tree ;
Rumors of song the stars may not endure ;
  A rain that falls and ceases suddenly.

Morn in thy garden, — bright and keen and
    strong !
  Love calls thee, from thy garden, to awake ;
Morn in thy garden, with the articulate song
  Of birds that sing for love and warm light's
    sake.

II.

Wind in thy garden to-night, my Love,
    Wind in thy garden and rain ;
A sound of storm in the shaken grove,
    And cries as of spirits in pain !

If there 's wind in thy garden outside,
    And troublous darkness, dear,
What carest thou, an elected bride,
    And the bridal hour so near ?

All things come to an end, my sweet, —
    Life, and the pleasure in living ;
The years run swiftly with agile feet,
    The years that are taking and giving.

Soon shalt thou have thy bliss supreme,
    And soon shall it pass away ;
So turn thyself to thy rest and dream,
    Nor heed what the mad winds say.

III.

Snow in thy garden, falling thick and fast,
  Snow in thy garden, where the grass shall be !
What dreams to-night? Thy dreaming nights
    are past ;
  Thou hast no glad or grievous memory.

Love in thy garden boweth down his head,
　His tears are falling on the wind-piled snow ;
He takes no heed of life, now thou art dead,
　He recks not how the seasons come or go.

Death in thy garden !   In the violent air
　That sweeps thy radiant garden thou art still ;
For thee is no more rapture or despair,
　And Love and Death of thee have had their
　　will.

Night in thy garden, white with snow and sleet ;
　Night rushing on with wind and storm toward
　　day, —
Alas ! thy garden holdeth nothing sweet,
　Nor sweet can come again, and *Thou* away.

—

University Press : John Wilson and Son, Cambridge.

STANDARD LIBRARY BOOKS

ROBERTS BROTHERS.

———◆———

Louisa M. Alcott. Little Women, Illustrated, 16mo, $1.50; Little Men, Illustrated, 16mo, $1.50; An Old-Fashioned Girl, Illustrated, 16mo, $1.50; Eight Cousins, Illustrated, 16mo, $1.50; Rose in Bloom, Illustrated, 16mo, $1.50; Under the Lilacs, Illustrated, 16mo, $1.50; Jack and Jill, Illustrated, 16mo, $1.50; Jo's Boys, Illustrated, 16mo, $1.50. Eight volumes in box, $12.00. Work, Illustrated, 16mo, $1.50, Moods, a Novel, 16mo, $1.50; Hospital Sketches, Illustrated, 16mo, $1.50.

A. Bronson Alcott. Table Talk, 16mo, $1.50; Concord Days, 16mo, $1.50; Record of a School, 16mo, $1.50; Tablets, with Portrait, 16mo, $1.50; Sonnets and Canzonets, 16mo, $1.00; New Connecticut, 16mo, $1.25.

William R. Alger. A Critical History of the Doctrine of a Future Life, 8vo, $3.50; The Genius of Solitude, 16mo, $1.50; The Friendships of Women, 16mo, $1.50; The School of Life, 16mo, $1.00; The Poetry of the Orient, Illustrated, 16mo, $1.50.

Joseph H. Allen. Hebrew Men and Times, 16mo, $1.50; Our Liberal Movement, 16mo, $1.25; Christian History in its Three Great Periods, 3 vols., 16mo, $3.75; Outlines of Christian History, 16mo, 75 cents.

Thomas G. Appleton. A Sheaf of Papers, 16mo, $1.50; A Nile Journey, Illustrated, 12mo, $2.25; Syrian Sunshine, 16mo, $1.00; Windfalls, Essays, 16mo, $1.50; Chequer Work, 16mo, $1.50.

Ernst Moritz Arndt. Life and Adventures of Arndt, with Portrait, 12mo, $2.25.

Edwin Arnold. The Light of Asia, 16mo, $1.00; Pearls of the Faith, 16mo, $1.00; Indian Idylls, 16mo, $1.00; The Secret of Death, 16mo, $1.00; The Song Celestial, 16mo, $1.00; India Revisited, Illustrated, 12mo, $2.00; Miscellaneous Poems, 16mo, $1.00.

W. P. Atkinson. On the Right Use of Books, 16mo, 50 cents; On History and the Study of History, 16mo, 50 cents.

Henry Bacon. A Parisian Year, Illustrated, 16mo, $1.50.

Honoré de Balzac. Père Goriot, 12mo, half Russia, $1.50; The Duchesse de Langeais, 12mo, half Russia, $1.50; César Birotteau, 12mo, half Russia, $1.50; Eugénie Grandet, 12mo, half Russia, $1.50; Cousin Pons, 12mo, half Russia, $1.50; The Country Doctor, 12mo, half Russia, $1.50; The Two Brothers, 12mo, half Russia, $1.50; The Alkahest, 12mo, half Russia, $1.50.

Anna Letitia Barbauld. Tales, Poems, and Essays. Biographical Sketch by Grace A. Oliver. 16mo, $1.00.

S Baring-Gould. Curious Myths of the Middle Ages, new edition, Illustrated, 16mo, $1.50.

William Barnes. Rural Poems, Illustrated, square 18mo, $1.25.

C A. Bartol, D. D. Radical Problems, 16mo, $1.25, The Rising Faith, 16mo, $1.25; Principles and Portraits, 16mo, $1.25.

William M. Baker. Blessed Saint Certainty, 16mo, $1.50; The Making of a Man, 16mo, $1.25, His Majesty, Myself, 16mo, $1.00.

Arlo Bates. Berries of the Brier (Poems), 16mo, $1.00; Sonnets in Shadow (Poems), 16mo, $1.00; A Lad's Love, a Story, 16mo, $1.00.

Henry Walter Bates. The Naturalist on the Amazon, Illustrated, 8vo, $2.50.

Karoline Bauer. Memoirs, from the German, 12mo, $1.50.

Walter Besant. The French Humorists, 12mo, $2.00; Studies in Early French Poetry, 12mo, $2.00.

William Blake. Poetical Works. With a Memoir by W. M. Rossetti. Portrait, 16mo, $2.25.

Mathilde Blind. Tarantella, a novel, 12mo, $1.50.

"Sherwood Bonner." Suwanee River Tales, Illustrated, 16mo. $1.25.

Mrs. E. V. Boyle. Days and Hours in a Garden, 16mo, white cloth, gilt, uncut, $2.00.

Mary Bradley. Hidden Sweetness, Illustrated, small 4to, $1.50.

Charles T. Brooks. Poems, with Memoir, 16mo, $1.25; William Ellery Channing, with Portrait, Illustrated, 16mo, $1.50; The Layman's Breviary, square 16mo, $1.50; The World-Priest, square 16mo, $2.25; The Wisdom of the Brahmin, 16mo, $1.25.

Sir Thomas Browne. Religio Medici, 16mo, $1.25.

Robert Buchanan. Poems, 16mo, $1.50.

Sir Edward Bulwer-Lytton. Dramas and Poems, with steel Portrait, square 18mo, $1.00; Schiller's Lay of the Bell, translated by Bulwer, Illustrated, oblong 4to, $7.50.

John Bunyan. The Pilgrim's Progress, Illustrated, 16mo, $1.00.

F. C. Burnand. Happy Thoughts, 16mo, $1.00; More Happy Thoughts, 16mo, $1.00; My Health, 16mo, $1.00; Happy Thought Hall, Illustrated, square 16mo, $2.00; The New History of Sandford and Merton, Illustrated, 16mo, $1.00; paper covers, 50 cents.

By The Tiber. A Novel, by the author of "Signor Monaldini's Niece," 16mo, $1.50.

T. Hall Caine. Recollections of D. G. Rossetti, with Portrait, 8vo, $3.00.

Helen Campbell. The What-to-do Club, 16mo, $1.50; Mrs. Herndon's Income, 16mo, $1.50; Miss Melinda's Opportunity, 16mo, $1.00; Prisoners of Poverty, 16mo, $1.00.

John W. Chadwick. Poems, 16mo, $1.00; In Nazareth Town, 16mo, $1.00; The Faith of Reason, 16mo, $1.00; The Man Jesus, 16mo, $1.00

Peleg W. Chandler. Memoir of Governor Andrew, Illustrated, 16mo. $1.25.

George L. Chaney. F. Grant & Co., Illustrated, 16mo, $1.00; Tom, Illustrated, 16mo, $1.00; Aloha, Illustrated, 16mo, $1.50; Every-day Life and Every-day Morals, 16mo, $1.00.

William Ellery Channing. Thoreau: the Poet-Naturalist, 16mo, $1.50.

Lydia Maria Child. Aspirations of the World, 16mo, $1.25.

P. W. Clayden. The Life of Samuel Sharpe, 12mo, $1.50.

"Mabel Collins." Through the Gates of Gold, a Fragment of Thought, 16mo, 50 cents.

Sara Coleridge. Phantasmion, 12mo, $2.00.

R. Laird Collier, D. D. Meditations on the Essence of Chris tianity, 12mo, $1.25.

"Susan Coolidge." The New Year's Bargain, Illustrated, 16mo, $1.25; What Katy Did, Illustrated, 16mo, $1.25; What Katy Did at School, Illustrated, 16mo, $1.25; What Katy Did Next, Illustrated, 16mo, $1.25; Mischief's Thanksgiving, Illustrated, 16mo, $1.25; Nine Little Goslings, Illustrated, 16mo, $1.25; Eyebright, Illustrated, 16mo, $1.25; Cross Patch, Illustrated, 16mo, $1.25; A Round Dozen, Illustrated, 16mo, $1.25; A Little Country Girl, Illustrated, 16mo, $1.25; A Guernsey Lily, Illustrated, 4to, $2.00; For Summer Afternoons, 16mo, $1.25; Short History of Philadelphia, 12mo, $1.25; Verses, square 16mo, $1.00.

Caroline H. Dall. Letters Home from Colorado, Utah, and California, 12mo, $1.50; What we Really Know about Shakespeare, second edition, 16mo, $1.25.

Madame D'Arblay. Diary and Letters, with Portraits, 2 vols., 12mo, $4.00.

J. Morrison Davidson. New Book of Kings, 16mo, $1.00.

Sir Humphry Davy. Consolations in Travel, Illustrated, 16mo, $1.50; Salmonia, Illustrated, $1.50.

Daniel Defoe. Robinson Crusoe, Illustrated, 12mo, $1.50.

Mrs. Delany. Autobiography, with Portraits, 2 vols., 12mo, $4.00.

Paul De Musset. Biography of Alfred De Musset, 12mo, $2.00.

Madame De Sévigné. Letters, 12mo, $1.50.

Orville Dewey. Autobiography, 12mo, $1.75.

George T. Dippold. The Great Epics of Mediæval Germany, 16mo, $1.50.

Anna Bowman Dodd. Cathedral Days, Illustrated, 12mo, $2.00.

Giovanni Duprè's Autobiographical Memoirs. With an Introduction by William W. Story. 12mo, $2.00.

Don Quixote, Wit and Wisdom of, Illustrated, 16mo, $1.25.

Dorothy. A Country Story in Verse, square 16mo, $1.25.

Samuel Adams Drake. Old Landmarks of Boston, Illustrated, 12mo, $2.00; Old Landmarks of Middlesex, Illustrated, 12mo, $2.00; New England Legends and Folk Lore, Illustrated, 8vo, $3.50; Around the Hub, Illustrated, 16mo, $1.50.

Maria Edgeworth. Classic Tales, 16mo, $1.00.

M. Betham Edwards. Doctor Jacob, a Novel, 12mo, $1.00.

George Eliot, Wit and Wisdom of, square 18mo, $1.00.

William Everett. School Sermons, 16mo, $1.00.

Famous Women Series. George Eliot, 16mo, $1.00; Emily Brontë, 16mo, $1.00; George Sand, 16mo, $1.00; Margaret Fuller, 16mo, $1.00; Mary Lamb, 16mo, $1.00; Maria Edgeworth, 16mo, $1.00; Elizabeth Fry, 16mo, $1.00; Mary Wollstonecraft, 16mo, $1.00; Harriet Martineau, 16mo, $1.00; Countess of Albany, 16mo, $1.00; Rachel Felix, 16mo, $1.00; Madame Roland, 16mo, $1.00; Mrs. Siddons, 16mo, $1.00; Margaret of Angoulême, 16mo, $1.00; Madame De Staël, 16mo, $1.00.

Festival Poems. For Christmas, etc. Square 16mo, $1.25.

Louis Figuier. To-morrow of Death, 16mo, $1.50.

"George Fleming." Kismet, 16mo, $1.00; Mirage, 16mo, $1.00; The Head of Medusa, 16mo, $1.50; Andromeda, 16mo, $1.50; Vestigia, 16mo, $1.25.

Mrs. Eliza Fletcher. Autobiography, with Portraits, 16mo, $1.50.

James E. Freeman. Gatherings from an Artist's Portfolio in Rome, 12mo, $1.50.

Ellen Frothingham's Translations. Goethe's Hermann and Dorothea, 16mo, $1.00; Illustrated, 8vo, $2.00; The Laocoön, 16mo, $1.50; Sappho, square 18mo, $1.00.

Margaret Fuller. Woman in the Nineteenth Century, 12mo, $1.50; Art, Literature, and the Drama, 12mo, $1.50; Life Without and Life Within, 12mo, $1.50; At Home and Abroad, 12mo, $1.50; Memoirs, 2 vols., 12mo, $3.00; Same, 1 vol., $1.50.

Theophile Gautier. My Household of Pets. Translated by "Susan Coolidge." Illustrated, 16mo, $1.25.

Judith Gautier. The Usurper, a Novel, 12mo, $1.50.

Oliver Goldsmith. The Vicar of Wakefield, with Illustrations by Mulready, 16mo, $1.00.

Lord Ronald Gower. My Reminiscences, with Portrait, 12mo, $2.00; Last Days of Marie Antoinette, with Portrait, small 4to, $4.00.

Louise Imogen Guiney. Goose-Quill Papers, 16mo, $1.00.

Edward Everett Hale. In His Name, Illustrated, 12mo, $2.00; square 18mo, $1.00; paper covers, 30 cents ; The Man Without a Country, 16mo, $1.25; His Level Best, 16mo, $1.25; What Career? 16mo, $1.25; The Ingham Papers, 16mo, $1.25; Christmas Eve and Christmas Day, 16mo, $1.25; Sybaris, 16mo, $1.25; Seven Spanish Cities, 16mo, $1.25; Ten Times One is Ten, 16mo, $1.00; Mrs. Merriam's Scholars, 16mo, $1.00; How to Do It, 16mo, $1.00; Good Time Coming, 16mo, $1.00; Gone to Texas, 16mo, $1.00; Crusoe in New York, 16mo, $1.00; Ups and Downs, 16mo, $1.50; A Summer Vacation, paper covers, 16mo, 50 cents; Franklin in France, with Portraits, 8vo, $3.00.

Eugenie Hamerton. The Mirror of Truth, Illustrated, 16mo, $2.00; Golden Mediocrity, 16mo, $1.00.

Philip G. Hamerton. A Painter's Camp, 12mo, $2.00; Thoughts about Art, 12mo, $2.00; Intellectual Life, 12mo, $2.00; Chapters on Animals, 12mo, $2.00; Round My House, 12mo, $2.00; The Sylvan Year and The Unknown River, 12mo, $2.00; Wenderholme, 12mo, $2.00; Modern Frenchmen, 12mo, $2.00; Life of J. M. W. Turner, 12mo, $2.00; The Graphic Arts, 12mo, $2.00; Human Intercourse, 12mo, $2.00; Landscape, 12mo, $2.00; Paris, Illustrated, 8vo, $3.00; Etching and Etchers, Illustrated, 8vo, $5.00; The Unknown River, Illustrated with etchings, 8vo, $6.00; Harry Blount, a Boy's Book, 16mo, $1.25.

Augustus J. C. Hare. Records of a Quiet Life, 16mo, $2.00.

The Heaven Series. Heaven Our Home, 16mo, $1.00; Life in Heaven, 16mo, $1.00; Meet for Heaven, 16mo, $1.00.

Lafcadio Hearn. Some Chinese Ghosts, 16mo, $1.00.

Frederic Henry Hedge. Primeval World of Hebrew Tradition, 16mo, $1.50; Reason in Religion, 16mo, $1.50; Ways of the Spirit, 16mo, $1.50; Atheism in Philosophy, 12mo, $2.00; Hours with German Classics, 8vo, $2.50

Arthur Helps. Companions of My Solitude, 16mo, $1.50; Essays, 16mo, $1.50; Brevia, 16mo, $1.50; Conversations on War and General Culture, 16mo, $1.50; Ivan de Biron, 12mo, $2.25; Thoughts Upon Government, 8vo, $2.25; Social Pressure, 8vo, $2.25; Brassey's Life, 8vo, $2.50; Realmah, 16mo, $2.00; Casimir Maremma, 16mo, $2.00.

Holy Songs, Carols, and Sacred Ballads, 16mo, $1.00.

F. L. Hosmer and W. C. Gannett. The Thought of God in Hymns and Poems, 16mo, $1.00; paper covers, 50 cents.

Lord Houghton. Poetical Works, with Portrait, 2 vols., 16mo, $5.00.

Julia Ward Howe. Margaret Fuller, 16mo, $1.00; Modern Society, 16mo, 50 cents.

Maud Howe. San Rosario Ranch, 16mo, $1.25; Atalanta in the South, 16mo, $1.25; A Newport Aquarelle, 16mo, $1.00.

Leigh Hunt. Book of the Sonnet, 16mo, $2.00; The Seer, 16mo, $2.00; A Day by the Fire, 16mo, $1.50.

Jean Ingelow. Poems, Cabinet edition, 16mo, $1.50; Diamond edition, square 18mo, $1.00; Household edition, 16mo, 75 cents; Red-Line Household edition, 12mo, $1.25; Illustrated edition, 8vo, $7.50; Birthday Book, Illustrated, 16mo, $1.00; Off the Skelligs, 16mo, $1.00; Fated to be Free, 16mo, $1.00; Sarah de Berenger, 16mo, $1.00; Don John, 16mo, $1.00, John Jerome, 16mo, $1.00; Poems of the Old Days and the New, 16mo, $1.25.

J. H. Ingraham. The Prince of the House of David, 16mo, $1.50; The Pillar of Fire, 16mo, $1.50; The Throne of David, 16mo, $1.50.

Helen Jackson. Ramona, 12mo, $1.50; Century of Dishonor, 12mo, $1.50; Glimpses of Three Coasts, 12mo, $1.50; Bits of Travel, Illustrated, 18mo, $1.25; Bits of Travel at Home, 18mo, $1.50; Bits of Talk, 18mo, $1.00; Bits of Talk for Young Folks. 16mo, $1.00; Mercy Philbrick's Choice, 16mo, $1.00; Hetty's Strange History, 16mo, $1.00; Zeph, 16mo, $1.25; Between Whiles, 16mo, $1.25; Verses, 16mo, $1.00; Sonnets and Lyrics, 16mo, $1.00; Verses and Sonnets and Lyrics, in 1 vol., $1.50.

Richard Jefferies. Wild Life in a Southern County, 16mo, $1.25 Gamekeeper at Home, 12mo, $1.50; Illustrated, 8vo, $3.75; The Amateur Poacher, 12mo, $1.50; Round About a Great Estate, 12mo, $1.50; Story of My Heart, 16mo, 75 cents.

Francis Jacox. Cues from All Quarters, 16mo, $1.50; Bible Music, 12mo, $1.75.

Joyce, R. D. Deirdré, a Poem, 16mo, $1.00; Blanid, a Poem, 16mo, $1.50.

Sylvester Judd. Margaret, 16mo, $1.50; Richard Edney, 16mo, $1.50.

John Keats. Poems. Memoir by Lord Houghton. 16mo, $1.50.

The Kernel and the Husk. Letters on Spiritual Christianity, by the author of "Philochristus" and "Onesimus," 12mo, $1.50.

Edward Lear. Nonsense Songs, Illustrated, 12mo, $1.25.

Walter Savage Landor. Pericles and Aspasia, 16mo, $1.50; Imaginary Conversations, 5 vols., 12mo, $10.00; Oxford edition, 16mo, $5.00.

Mrs. E. W. Latimer. Familiar Talks on Some of Shakspeare's Comedies, 12mo, $2.00.

Vernon Lee. Baldwin, 12mo, $2.00; Euphorion, 2 vols., demy 8vo, $4.00; Countess of Albany, 16mo, $1.00; A Phantom Lover, 16mo, 50 cents; Juvenilia, 12mo, $2.00.

Madame Lenormant. Memoirs of Madame Récamier, with Portrait, 16mo, $1.50; Madame Récamier and Her Friends, 16mo, $1.50.

Mrs. D. A. Lincoln. Boston Cook Book, Illustrated, 12mo, half bound, $2.00; Carving and Serving, square 12mo, 60 cents.

W. J. Linton. Rare Poems of Sixteenth and Seventeenth Centuries, 16mo, $2.00.

A Little Pilgrim, 16mo, 60 cents.

Abiel A. Livermore. Anti-Tobacco, 16mo, 50 cents.

Living English Poets (MDCCCLXXXII), 12mo, $2.00.

Margaret Lonsdale. Sister Dora, with Portrait, 16mo, $1.25.

Robert T. S. Lowell. Antony Brade, 16mo, $1.75; A Story or Two from an Old Dutch Town, 16mo, $1.25.

W. M. Lupton. A Concise English History, 12mo, $1.50.

Hamilton W. Mabie. Norse Stories, 16mo, $1.00.

Lord Macaulay. Lays of Ancient Rome, with "Ivry" and "Armada," Illustrated, 16mo, $1.00.

John MacGregor. Thousand Miles in the Rob Roy Canoe, 16mo, $1.25; Rob Roy on the Baltic, 16mo, $1.25; Voyage Alone in the Yawl Rob Roy, 16mo, $1.25; Three vols. in one, $2.00.

George MacDonald. The Vicar's Daughter, Illustrated, 16mo, $1.50.

Gerardine Macpherson. Memoirs of Anna Jameson, with Portrait, 8vo, $2.50.

James Martineau. Hours of Thought on Sacred Things, 1st series, 16mo, $1.50; 2d series, 12mo, $2.00.

George Meredith. Ordeal of Richard Feverel, uncut, English cloth, 12mo, $2.00; Evan Harrington, uncut, English cloth, 12mo, $2.00; Harry Richmond, uncut, English cloth, 12mo, $2.00; Sandra Belloni, uncut, English cloth, 12mo, $2.00; Vittoria, uncut, English cloth, 12mo, $2.00; Rhoda Fleming, uncut, English cloth, 12mo, $2.00; Beauchamp's Career, uncut, English cloth, 12mo, $2.00; Diana of the Crossways, uncut, English cloth, 12mo, $2.00; The Egoist, uncut, English cloth, 12mo, $2.00; Shaving of Shagpat, and Farina, uncut, English cloth, 12mo, $2.00; Ballads and Poems of Tragic Life, 16mo, $1.50.

Joaquin Miller. Songs of the Sierras, 16mo, $1.50; Songs of the Sun Lands, 16mo, $1.50; Ship in the Desert, 16mo, $1.50; Songs of Italy, 16mo, $1.25; Four vols. in one, $2.00; Songs of the Mexican Seas, 16mo, $1.00.

Miss Toosey's Mission, and Laddie, 1 vol., 16mo, 50 cents.

J. L. Molloy. Our Autumn Holiday on French Rivers, 16mo, $1.00.

Lady Mary Wortley Montagu. Letters, 12mo, $1.50.

John Morley. Life of Richard Cobden, with Portrait, 8vo, $1.50.

Lewis Morris. The Epic of Hades, 16mo, $1.50; Gwen, 16mo, $1.50; Songs Unsung, 16mo, $1.50; The Ode of Life, 16mo, $1.00.

William Morris. The Earthly Paradise, 3 vols., 16mo, gilt, $6.00; Popular edition, $4.50; Sigurd the Volsung, 8vo, $2.50; Æneids of Virgil, 8vo, $2.50; Defence of Guenevere, 12mo, $2.00; Life and Death of Jason, 16mo, $1.50; Lovers of Gudrun, 16mo, $1.00; Love is Enough, 16mo, $1.25; Hopes and Fears for Art, 16mo, $1.25.

Louise Chandler Moulton. Poems, square 18mo, $1.00; Some Women's Hearts, 16mo, $1.50; Random Rambles, 18mo, $1.25; Ourselves and Our Neighbors, 16mo, $1.00.

William A. Mowry. Talks with My Boys, 16mo, $1.00.

My Marriage. A Novel, 16mo, $1.00.

May Alcott Nieriker. Studying Art Abroad, 16mo, 50 cents.

No Name Novels. *First Series:* Afterglow, $1.00; Deirdrè, $1.00; Is That All? $1.00; Will Denbigh, Nobleman, $1.00; Kismet, $1.00; Wolf at the Door, $1.00; The Great Match, $1.00; Marmorne, $1.00; Mirage, $1.00; A Modern Mephistopheles, $1.00; Gemini, $1.00; A Masque of Poets, $1.00.

Second Series: Signor Monaldini's Niece, $1.00; The Colonel's Opera Cloak, $1.00; His Majesty, Myself, $1.00; Mrs. Beauchamp Brown, $1.00; Salvage, $1.00; Don John, $1.00; Tsar's Window, $1.00; Manuela Parédes, $1.00; Baby Rue, $1.00; My Wife and My Wife's Sister, $1.00; Her Picture, $1.00; Aschenbroedel, $1.00.

Third Series: Her Crime, $1.00; Little Sister, $1.00; Barrington's Fate, $1.00; Daughter of the Philistines, $1.00; Princess Amélie, $1.00; Diane Coryval, $1.00; Almost a Duchess, $1.00; A Superior Woman, $1.00; Justina, $1.00; Question of Identity, $1.00; Cracker Joe, $1.00.

Mrs. Power O'Donoghue. Riding for Ladies, 12mo, $3.50.

Old Lady Mary. A Tale of the Seen and the Unseen, 16mo, 60 cents.

Kathleen O'Meara. Madame Mohl, 16mo, $1.25 (crown 8vo, $2.50); Mabel Stanhope, 16mo, $1.25.

Old Colony Series of Novels. Constance of Acadia, 12mo, $1.50; Agatha and the Shadow, 12mo, $1.50.

Onesimus, Memoirs of a Disciple of Saint Paul, 16mo, $1.50.

Open Door and The Portrait, 1 vol., 16mo, 60 cents.

Dr. H. Oort and Dr. I. Hooykaas. The Bible for Learners, 3 vols., 12mo, $6.00.

John Boyle O'Reilly. Moondyne, a Novel, 16mo, $1.00; Statues in the Block, 16mo, $1.00; paper covers, 50 cents.

Our Little Ann. By the author of " Tip Cat." 16mo, $1.00.

Joseph Parker, D. D. Ecce Deus, 16mo, $1.00; Ad Clerum, 16mo, $1.50.

Theodore Parker. Prayers, 16mo, $1.00; Lessons from the World of Matter, 12mo, $1.25.

Charles E. Pascoe. London of To-day, 1887, Illustrated, 12mo, $1.50.

C. Kegan Paul. William Godwin, 2 vols., 8vo, $6.00; Mary Wollstonecraft's Letters to Gilbert Imlay, square 12mo, $2.00.

Paul of Tarsus, 16mo, $1.50.

Elizabeth P. Peabody. Reminiscences of William Ellery Channing, 16mo, $2.00.

A. P. Peabody, D. D. Christian Belief and Life, 16mo, $1.50.

Frances M. Peard. The Rose Garden, 16mo, $1.50; Thorpe Regis, 16mo, $1.50; Unawares, 16mo, $1.50.

Silvio Pellico. My Prisons, Illustrated, 16mo, $1.25.

"Pembridge." Whist, or Bumblepuppy? 16mo, 50 cents.

J. and E. R. Pennell. Two Pilgrims' Progress, Illustrated, 12mo, $2.00; paper covers, 50 cents.

Philochristus, Memoirs of a Disciple of Our Lord, 16mo, $1.50.

Edward L. Pierce. Memoir and Letters of Charles Sumner, with Portraits, 2 vols., 8vo, $6.00.

Margaret J. Preston. Cartoons, 16mo, $1.00.

Laura Elizabeth Poor. Sanskrit and its Kindred Literatures, 16mo, $2.00.

Harriet W. Preston. A Year in Eden, a Novel, 12mo, $1.50; Troubadours and Trouvères, 12mo, $2.00; Aspendale, 16mo, $1.00; Love in Nineteenth Century, 16mo, $1.00; Translations: Mistral's Mirèio, 16mo, $1.25; Writings of Madame Swetchine, 16mo, $1.25; Life and Letters of Madame Swetchine, 16mo, $1.50; Portraits of Celebrated Women, 16mo, $1.50; Memoirs of Madame Desbordes-Valmore, 16mo, $1.50; Biography of Alfred de Musset, 12mo, $2.00.

Bryan Waller Procter. An Autobiographical Fragment, with Portrait, 12mo, $2.00.

Alfred P. Putnam. Singers and Songs of the Liberal Faith, 8vo, $3.00.

Josiah Quincy. Figures of the Past, 16mo, $1.50.

Josiah P. Quincy. Protection of Majorities, 16mo, $1.00.

Harriet H. Robinson. Massachusetts in the Woman Suffrage Movement, 16mo, $1.25.

A. Mary F. Robinson. The New Arcadia, 16mo, $1.50; An Italian Garden, 16mo, $1.00; Emily Brontë, 16mo, $1.00.

Phil. Robinson. Under the Sun, 16mo, $1.50; Sinners and Saints: Three Months Among the Mormons, 16mo, $1.50.

Edwards Roberts. Santa Barbara, Illustrated, 16mo, 75 cents.

Christina G. Rossetti. Poems, 16mo, $1.50; Red Line edition, 12mo, $2.00; A Pageant, 16mo, $1.25; Time Flies, 18mo, $1.00; Annus Domini, square 18mo, $1.50; Commonplace, 16mo, $1.50.

Dante Gabriel Rossetti. Blessed Damozel, 16mo, $1.50; Ballads and Sonnets, 16mo, $1.50; Complete Poems, with Portrait, 12mo, $2.00; Dante and His Circle, 12mo, $2.00.

Maria Francesca Rossetti. A Shadow of Dante, Illustrated, 12mo, $1.50.

Earl John Russell. Recollections, 8vo, $3.00.

Bernardin de Sainte-Pierre. Paul and Virginia, Illustrated, 16mo, $1.00.

C. A. Sainte-Beuve. Portraits of Celebrated Women, 16mo, $1.50; Memoirs of Madame Desbordes-Valmore, 16mo, $1.50.

Frank B. Sanborn. Life and Letters of John Brown, with Portraits, 8vo, $3.00.

George Sand. Mauprat, 12mo, half Russia, $1.50; Antonia, 12mo, half Russia, $1.50; Monsieur Sylvestre, 12mo, half Russia, $1.50; Snow Man, 12mo, half Russia, $1.50; Miller of Angibault, 12mo, half Russia, $1.50.

Epes Sargent. Planchette; or, The Despair of Science, 16mo, $1.25; The Woman who Dared, 16mo, $1.50.

Sir Walter Scott. Lay of the Last Minstrel, Lady of the Lake, and Marmion, 1 vol., 16mo, $1.00.

Sea and Shore, a Collection of Poems, 18mo, $1.00.

J. R. Seeley, M. A. Ecce Homo, 16mo, $1.00; Roman Imperialism, 16mo, $1.50; Short History of Napoleon, with Portrait, 16mo, $1.50; Life and Times of Stein, 2 vols., with Portrait, 8vo, $6.00; Natural Religion, 16mo, $1.25; Expansion of England, crown 8vo, $1.75.

Flora L. Shaw. Colonel Cheswick's Campaign, a Novel, 16mo, $1.25; Castle Blair, 16mo, $1.00; Hector, 16mo, $1.00; Phyllis Browne, 16mo, $1.00; A Sea Change, 16mo, $1.00.

Six of One by Half-a-Dozen of the Other, 16mo, $1.50.

Julian K. Smyth. Footprints of the Saviour, 16mo, gilt top, $1.00.

Mary Somerville. Personal Recollections, Portrait, 12mo, $1.50.

Robert Southey. Life of Nelson, Illustrated, 16mo, $1.00.

Harriet Prescott Spofford. The Marquis of Carabas, 16mo, $1.00; Hester Stanley at St. Marks, 12mo, $1.25.

"A Square." Flatland, Illustrated, 16mo, 75 cents.

Robert Louis Stevenson. Travels with a Donkey, 16mo, $1.00; An Inland Voyage, 16mo, $1.00; Treasure Island, 16mo, $1.00; The Silverado Squatters, 16mo, $1.00; Prince Otto, 16mo, $1.00.

Harriet Beecher Stowe. Pink and White Tyranny, 16mo, $1.25.

Charles Swain. Poems, with Portrait, 18mo, $1.00.

Andrew James Symington. William Wordsworth, with Portrait, 2 vols., 16mo, $2.00.

Jane and Ann Taylor. Tales, Essays, and Poems. Biographical Sketch, by Grace A. Oliver. 16mo, $1.00.

Connop Thirlwall. Letters to a Friend, 12mo, $1.50.

Mary W. Tileston. Quiet Hours, 1st Series, 16mo, $1.00; 2d Series, 16mo, $1.00; 2 vols. in one, $1.50; Sursum Corda, 16mo, $1.25; The Blessed Life, 18mo, $1.00; Daily Strength for Daily Needs, 16mo, $1.00; Heroic Ballads, Illustrated, 12mo, $2.00; "The Wisdom Series," comprising The Apocrypha, 18mo, flexible covers, 50 cents; Ecclesiasticus, 18mo, flexible covers, 50 cents; Marcus Aurelius Antoninus, 18mo, flexible covers, 50 cents; The Imitation of Christ, 18mo, flexible covers, 50 cents; Sunshine in the Soul, 1st Series, 18mo, flexible covers, 50 cents; 2d Series, 18mo, flexible covers, 50 cents (both in one, 75 cents); Epictetus, 18mo, flexible covers, 50 cents; Life of Dr. John Tauler, 18mo, flexible covers, 50 cents; Selections from Fénelon, 18mo, flexible covers, 50 cents; Socrates, 2 vols., 18mo, flexible covers, 50 cents each. In sets, complete in six volumes, $4.50.

Tip Cat, A Story. By the author of "Miss Toosey's Mission." 16mo, $1.00.

George M. Towle. Certain Men of Mark, 16mo, $1.00.

W. Steuart Trench. Realities of Irish Life, 12mo, $1.00.

R. St. John Tyrwhitt. Our Sketching Club, Illustrated, 8vo, $2.50.

Sarah Tytler. The Old Masters, 16mo, $1.50; Modern Painters, 16mo, $1.50; Musical Composers, 16mo, $1.50.

May Alden Ward. Dante, a Sketch of his Life, 16mo, $1.25.

M. de Voltaire. Charles XII., King of Sweden, with Portrait, 16mo, $1.00.

William B. Weeden. Morality of Prohibitory Liquor Laws, 16mo, $1.25; The Social Law of Labor, 12mo, $1.50.

Rev. John Weiss. American Religion, 16mo, $1.50; Wit, Humor, and Shakspeare, 12mo, $2.00.

Oscar Wilde. Poems, 16mo, $1.25.

A Week Away from Time, 16mo, $1.25.

Rev. J. G. Wood. Nature's Teachings, Illustrated, 8vo, $2.50.

Abba Goold Woolson. Dress Reform, Illustrated, 16mo, $1.50; Browsing Among Books, 16mo, $1.00.

Benjamin Worcester. Life and Mission of Emanuel Swedenborg, with Portrait, 12mo, $2.00 (8vo, $3.00).

LATEST ADDITIONS TO ROBERTS BROTHERS' CATALOGUE.

Albion W. Tourgee. Button's Inn, a Story, 16mo, $1.25.

Philip Bourke Marston. For a Song's Sake, and Other Stories, 12mo, $2.00 ; Garden Secrets, with a Sketch of his Life by Louise Chandler Moulton, and Portrait, 16mo, $1.00.

Esther Bernon Carpenter. South-County Neighbors, 16mo, $1.00.

William Shakespeare. Complete Works, Dyce's Edition, 7 vols., 16mo, half Russia, in a neat box, $9.00.

Laura E. Richards. Toto's Joyous Winter, a continuation of "The Joyous Story of Toto," 16mo, $1.25.

Louisa M. Alcott. A Garland for Girls, and Other Stories, uniform with "Spinning-Wheel Stories," 16mo, $1.25 ; Lulu's Library, Vol. II., uniform with Lulu's Library, Vol. I., 16mo, $1.00.

Edward E. Hale. In His Name, a new edition, with more than 100 Illustrations by G. P. Jacomb-Hood, R.A., 12mo, $2.00.

Philip Gilbert Hamerton. The Saône, a Summer Voyage, with 150 Illustrations by Joseph Pennell and the author, 4to. (*In the press.*)

The Little Flowers of Saint Francis. Translated by Abby Langdon Alger. 16mo, 75 cents.

T. S. Millington. Some of Our Fellows, a School Story, with 16 Illustrations, small 4to, $2.00.

Joaquin Miller. Songs of the Mexican Seas, comprising The Sea of Fire and The Rhyme of the Great River, 16mo, $1.00.

George Meredith. Ballads and Poems of Tragic Life, 16mo, $1.50.

Vernon Lee. Juvenilia: being a Second Series of Essays on Sundry Æsthetical Questions, uniform with " Baldwin " (the First Series), 12mo, $2.00.

Madame de Staël. A Life of this celebrated woman, the author of "Corinne," being the 15th Volume in the Famous Women Series, 16mo, $1.00.

Send for Descriptive Catalogue of our Publications (free).
All of our Books are mailed, post-paid, on receipt of price.

ROBERTS BROTHERS, Publishers,

3 SOMERSET STREET, BOSTON.